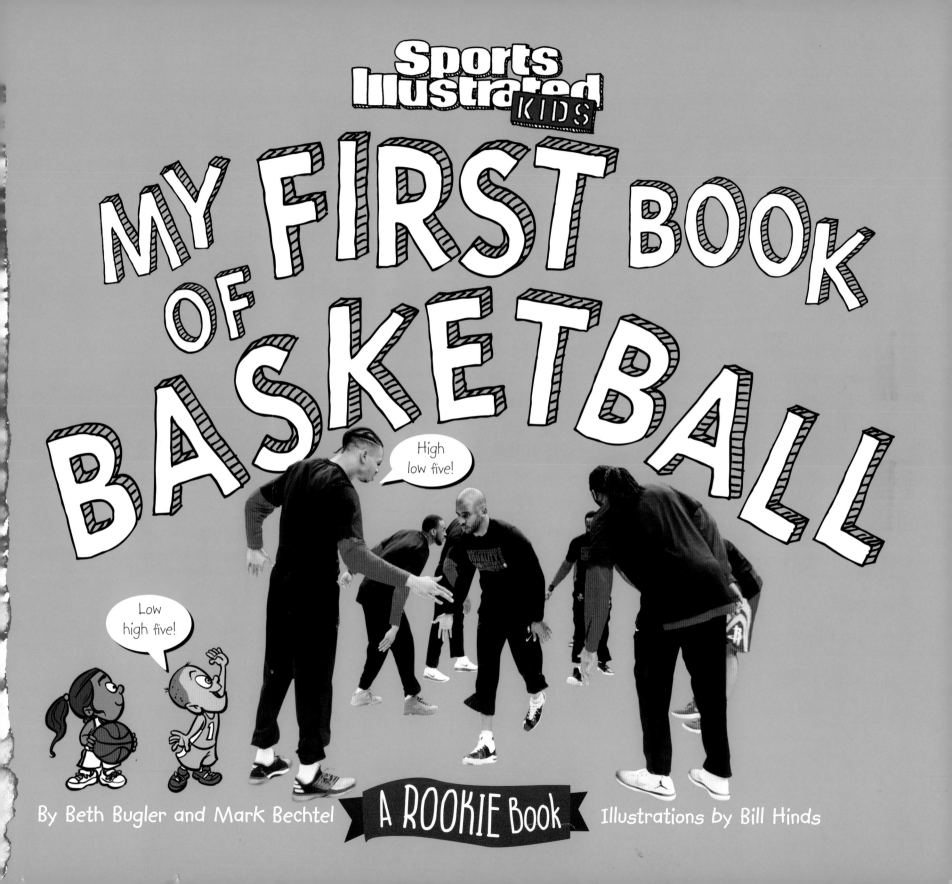

The game is divided into

FOUR QUARTERS

that are **12 MINUTES** long.

After the second quarter, the teams take a

HALFTIME

break so the players can rest.

And the fans can make a pit stop?

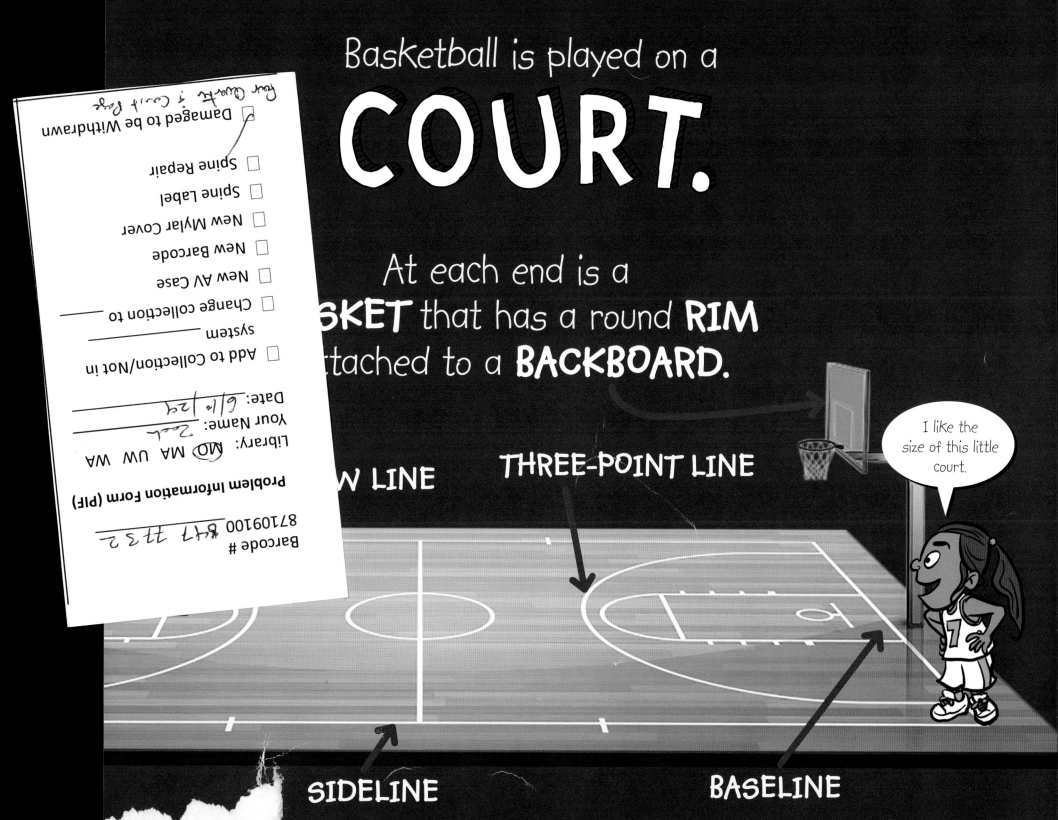

Basketball is played on a

COURT.

At each end is a **...SKET** that has a round **RIM** ...tached to a **BACKBOARD.**

...W LINE

THREE-POINT LINE

I like the size of this little court.

SIDELINE

BASELINE

The five team
members have
different duties.

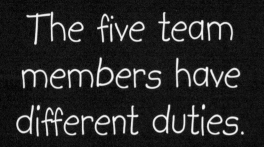

POINT GUARD: A little guy with a big job. He's like a coach on the court, telling players what to do.

SHOOTING GUARD: A good scorer who can shoot the ball through the basket.

SMALL FORWARD: A versatile player who needs to be big and strong, but also quick.

POWER FORWARD: A big, tough guy who can score and also guard opposing players.

CENTER: Usually the tallest guy on the team. He tends to hang out near the basket.

Two players face off and the

REFEREE

tosses the ball in the air.

That was my best toss ever!

The players jump and try to tap the ball to a teammate.

The team that has the ball is called the **OFFENSE.**

The team that is trying to stop them from scoring is called the **DEFENSE.**

Players move the ball around by throwing a

to a teammate.

What? Did you think I wasn't going to catch it?

The offense can also move the ball around the court by

DRIBBLING.

A player bounces the ball up and down with one hand.

Could this be a cool dance move?

TIME
9:54

If a player takes more than two steps without dribbling, the referee will call

TRAVELING,

and the team that was on defense gets the ball.

My family travels a lot. Do you have a signal for going to the beach?

The offense has to shoot the ball before the

SHOT CLOCK

runs out. In men's games, that's 24 seconds. In women's games, it's 30.

Looks good . . .

. . . doesn't look good.

No! The shot clangs off the rim. Now the players try to grab the

REBOUND.

A defensive player snatches the ball, and now his team is on offense.

Looks good!

. . . and gets off a shot.

SWISH!

The ball goes through the hoop.

Two points!

The team that gave up the basket now gets possession of the ball behind the baseline. They have to make an

INBOUNDS PASS.

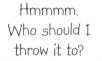

Hmmmm. Who should I throw it to?

I'm open!

It's a new quarter and a guard is dribbling the ball up the court.

Coach is going to be so disappointed in me.

Look out! The defensive player reaches in and takes the ball away. It's a

STEAL!

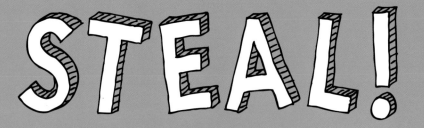

Just **try** and get this away from me.

But you have to be careful when you're trying for a steal. If one player makes too much contact with another, the referee will blow the whistle and call a

FOUL.

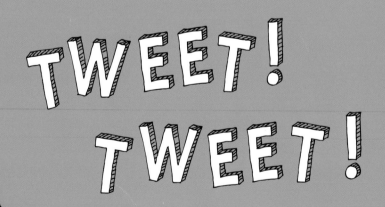

TWEET!
TWEET!

Certain fouls lead to

FREE THROWS.

The player who was fouled shoots from the free throw line, and the defensive players can't guard her.

A free throw that goes in the basket is worth one point.

You know what *else* is free? A hug!

Since he's behind the
three-point line, the shot is a

THREE-POINTER.

It's worth an extra point if it goes in!

:54

Yes! Three points!

BZZZZZZZ!

There's the buzzer.
That means it's . . .

We're back in action.
A player is taking a shot
near the basket.

But the defensive team's center
comes over and

BLOCKS

the shot.

She knocks the
shot away!

Here's my
blocking
technique.

QUARTER

3RD

Hey, can you do me a solid? My dogs are barking!

Somebody looks like he's getting tired. It's time for a

SUBSTITUTION.

Anytime there's a break in play, a new player can come onto the floor and replace a teammate.

I got you, bro.

If we sit here, maybe they will accidentally send us in.

TIME
8:22

Play starts up again. The referee calls

GOALTENDING.

That's when a player knocks away a shot that is on its way down into the basket. You can only block a shot when the ball is on the way up.

The referee blows his whistle and the shot counts as a made basket.

Uh-oh. This guy doesn't agree with the referee's call. He complains too much, and the referee calls a

TECHNICAL FOUL.

The other team gets to shoot a free throw.

When I complain too much, I get sent to my room.

A player grabs a loose ball and starts dribbling as fast as he can toward the other team's basket. It's a

FAST BREAK.

His teammates run with him, and the defense tries to catch up. Will they get him?

No! It's a

SLAM DUNK!

He rises up and stuffs the
ball through the hoop!

Wow.

How does
he get down
from there?

It's getting late and the game is close. The coach calls a

The players gather around and the coach draws up a play.

They go back on the court.

Look! My play has a dragon!

The seconds
tick off.
Four.
Three.
Two.
One.

He launches
a shot just
before time
runs out.
It goes in!

The two points give his team the win!

GAME OVER!

It's time to celebrate!

I thought this might come in handy!

Writers: Beth Bugler, Mark Bechtel
Designer: Beth Bugler
Illustrator: Bill Hinds
Production Manager: Hillary Leary

Published by Liberty Street,
an imprint of
Time Inc. Books
225 Liberty Street
New York, NY 10281

ISBN: 978-1-5478-0002-5
Library of Congress Control Number: 2018942109

First edition, 2018
1 TLF 18
10 9 8 7 6 5 4 3 2 1

We welcome your comments and suggestions
about Time Inc. Books. Please write to us at:
Time Inc. Books
Attention: Book Editors
P.O. Box 62310
Tampa, FL 33662-2310
(800) 765-6400

timeincbooks.com

Time Inc. Books products may be purchased for
business or promotional use. For information on
bulk purchases, please contact Christi Crowley in
the Special Sales Department at (845) 895-9858.

PHOTO CREDITS, in order:
Dan Thornberg/EyeEm/Getty Images (cover);
Jason Miller/Getty Images (title page);
Noah Graham/Getty Images,
Daniel Gluskoter/Icon Sportswire/Getty Images
(two teams); Jason Miller/Getty Images (2),
Michael J. LeBrecht II/NBAE/Getty Images (2),
David Liam Kyle/NBAE/Getty Images (five
players); Getty Images (court); Nathaniel S. Butler/
NBAE/Getty Images (five team members); Glenn
James/NBAE/Getty Images (tip-off);
Mark Sobhani/NBAE/Getty Images (offense,
pass); Hannah Foslien/Getty Images (dribbling);
Doug Pensinger/Getty Images (traveling);
Ned Dishman/NBAE/Getty Images (shot clock);
Andrew D. Bernstein/NBAE/Getty Images
(rebound); Jesse D. Garrabrant/NBAE/Getty
Images (swish, inbounds pass); Ryan McVay/Getty
Images (net); Matthew J. Lee/The Boston Globe/
Getty Images (steal); Corey Perrine/Getty Images
(foul); Tony Quinn/Icon Sportswire/Corbis/Getty
Images (not gentle); Ned Dishman/NBAE/Getty
Images (free throws); Sam Forencich/NBAE/Getty
Images (three-pointer); Jonathan Bachman/Getty
Images (net); Fernando Medina/NBAE/Getty
Images (Magic); Ron Turenne/NBAE/Getty Images
(Raptors); Garrett Ellwood/NBAE/Getty Images
(Nuggets) (halftime); Scott Cunningham/NBAE/
Getty Images (blocks); Layne Murdoch/NBAE/
Getty Images, Timothy Nwachukwu/Getty Images
(substitution); Matthew J. Lee/The Boston Globe/
Getty Images (goaltending); Peter Zay/Anadolu
Agency/Getty Images, David Liam Kyle/NBAE/
Getty Images (technical foul); Mike McGinnis/
Getty Images (fast break); Greg Nelson (slam
dunk); Matteo Marchi/Getty Images (timeout);
Vaughn Ridley/Getty Images (buzzer beater);
Garrett Ellwood/NBAE/Getty Images (game over);
Jonathan Bachman/Getty Images (back cover)